W9-AZW-660

No Longer Property of the
Fayetteville Public Library

FAYETTEVILLE PUBLIC LIBRARY
401 W MOUNTAIN ST.
FAYETTEVILLE, AR 72701

09/15/2009

Learning About Life Cycles
The Life Cycle of a
Ladybug

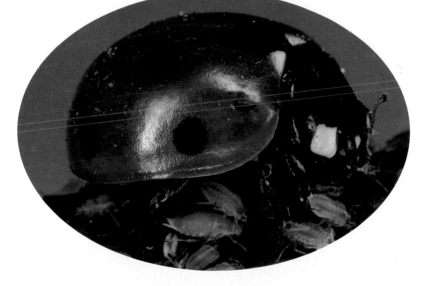

Ruth Thomson

press.

New York

Published in 2009 by The Rosen Publishing Group Inc.
29 East 21st Street, New York, NY 10010

Copyright © 2009 Wayland/The Rosen Publishing Group, Inc.

All rights reserved. No part of this book may be reproduced in any form without permission from the publisher, except by a reviewer.

First Edition

Editor: Victoria Brooker
Designer: Simon Morse
Consultant: Michael Scott OBE, B.Sc

Library of Congress Cataloging-in-Publication Data

Thomson, Ruth, 1949-
  The life cycle of a ladybug / Ruth Thomson. — 1st ed.
     p. cm. — (Learning about life cycles)
  Includes index.
  ISBN 978-1-4358-2835-3 (library binding)
  ISBN 978-1-4358-2885-8 (paperback)
  ISBN 978-1-4358-2891-9 (6-pack)
  1. Ladybugs—Life cycles—Juvenile literature. I. Title.
  QL596.C65T46 2009
  595.76'9—dc22
                                        2008025780

Manufactured in China

Photographs: Cover (tr), 10 blickwinkel/Alamy; Cover (main), 6 blickwinkel/Kottmann/Alamy; Cover (br), 1, 15, 23 (br) Andrew Darrington/ Alamy; 2 Redmond Durrell/Alamy; 11 Holt Studios International Ltd/Alamy; 8 Juniors Bildarchiv/Alamy; 12 Mercer/insects/Alamy; 17 Papilio/Alamy; 7 WoodyStock/Alamy; 3, 4, 5, 6, 8, 9, 13, 14, 16, 18, 19, 20, 21, 22, 23 naturepl.com

Web Sites

Due to the changing nature of Internet links, PowerKids Press has developed an online list of Web sites related to the subject of this book. This site is updated regularly. Please use this link to access this list: www.powerkidslinks.com/lalc/ladybug

Contents

Ladybugs live here

Ladybugs live in yards, parks, forests, and fields. They eat tiny **aphids** that live on plants.

What is a ladybug?

A ladybug is an **insect** with a hard skin that protects it. Its bright color warns birds that it tastes nasty.

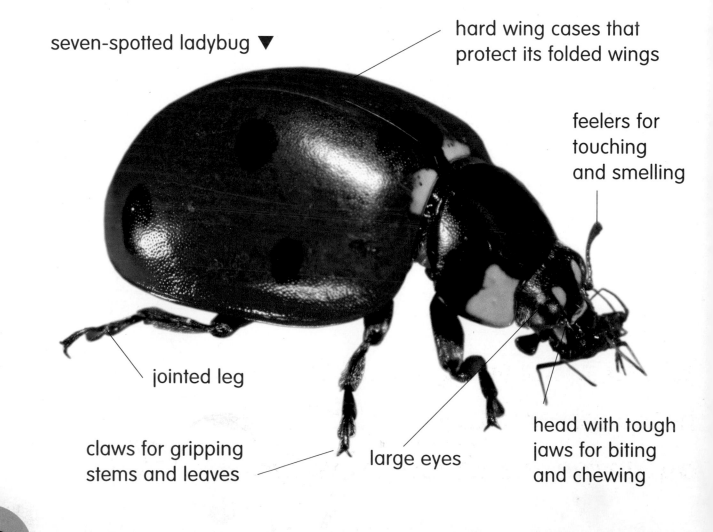

seven-spotted ladybug ▼

hard wing cases that protect its folded wings

feelers for touching and smelling

jointed leg

claws for gripping stems and leaves

large eyes

head with tough jaws for biting and chewing

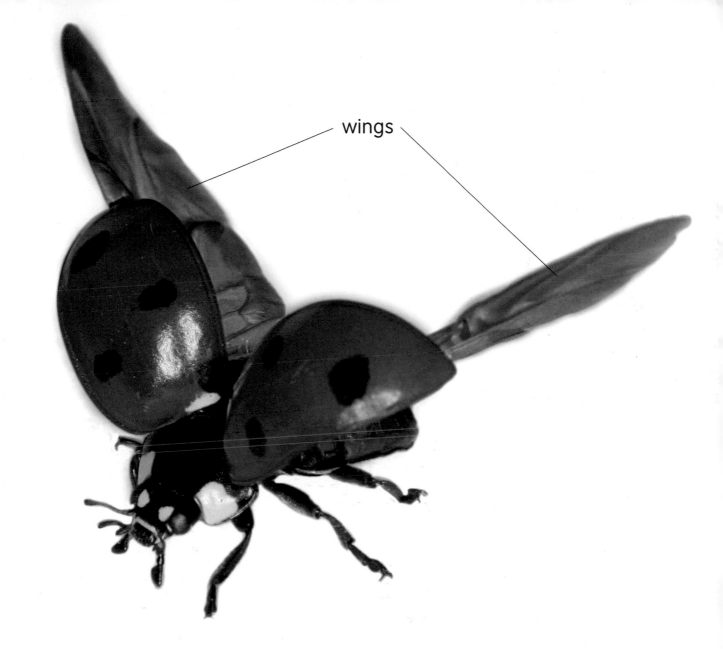

wings

When a ladybug flies, it lifts
its spotty wing cases and fans
out large see-through wings.

Time to lay eggs

In the spring, the male ladybug looks for a female. He finds her by her special smell. The ladybugs **mate**.

A week later, the female lays lots of sticky eggs. She lays them in groups on plants where **aphids** live.

Hatching

After a few days, a tiny **larva** **hatches** from each egg. At first, it is white. Soon it turns black.

The larva feeds on **aphids**.
It is hungry all the time.
As it grows bigger,
its skin becomes too tight.

1 week

Molting

The tight skin splits and comes off. This is called **molting**. The **larva** has new skin underneath. It molts three more times as it grows.

The larva eats about 30 **aphids** a day. It sucks the juices out of them through its hollow tongue. The larva grows even bigger.

2-3
weeks

Pupa

The fat **larva** stops eating. It fixes its tail to a stem with sticky glue. Its skin splits for the last time. There is a **pupa** inside.

3-4 weeks

The pupa hangs completely still. Inside its hard case, the pupa changes into an adult ladybug.

Adult ladybug

Soon, the ladybug is ready
to come out. It pushes
itself head first out of the case.
Its body is soft, pale, and damp.

5 weeks

The ladybug rests until its body hardens. It opens its wings so they dry out. Soon, its spots and red color appear.

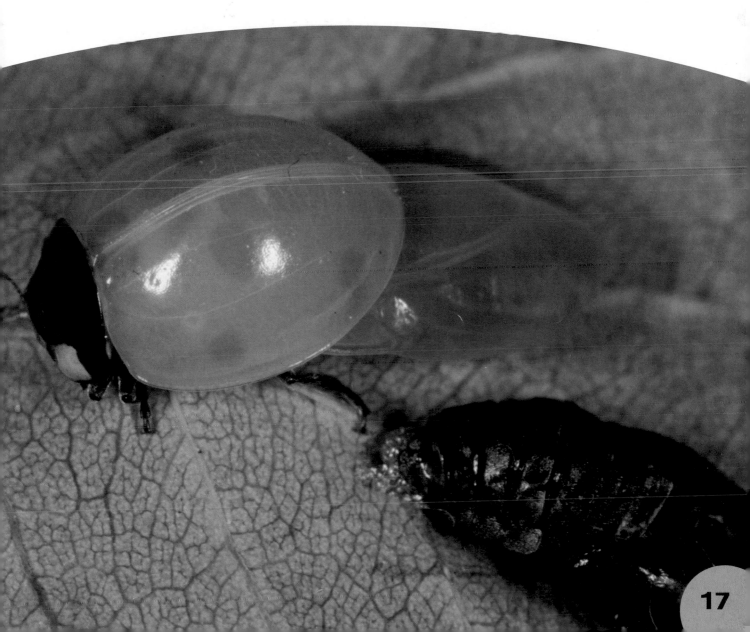

 # Feeding

The ladybug flies from plant to plant all summer eating **aphids**.

18

The ladybug also sips **nectar** from flowers. The nectar gives it energy for flying.

Sleeping through winter

When the weather turns colder, there are fewer **aphids** around. Ladybugs crowd together in a sheltered place. They sleep there all winter long.

Ready to mate

In the spring, when the weather warms up, the ladybug wakes up. It flies away to look for food and to **mate**. The female will lay new eggs.

Ladybug life cycle

Eggs
In the spring, the ladybug lays eggs in groups of 10 to 50 on leaves.

Larva
The **larva** hatches and eats **aphids** for three to four weeks.

Adult ladybug
After a week, an adult ladybug comes out of the pupa.

Pupa
The larva becomes a **pupa**.

Glossary and Further Information

aphid a tiny insect, such as greenfly and blackfly, that feeds on plants

hatch to come out of an egg

insect a small creature with six legs, a three-part body—head, thorax, and abdomen—and a pair of feelers

larva an insect in its first stage after coming out of an egg

mate when a male and female join together to produce young

molting shedding skin (or hair or feathers)

nectar the sweet liquid inside many flowers

pupa the form that an insect takes when it changes from a larva into an adult

Books

Animal Life Cycles
by Bobbie Kalman (Crabtree Publishing, 2006)

Life Cycles: Ladybug
by David M Schwartz (Gareth Stevens Publishing, 2001)

Index